SUMMARY OF HEARING GOD'S VOICE FOR HEALING

Practical Paths to Divine Health

MARK VIRKLER

PATTI VIRKLER

DESTINY IMAGE

Destiny Image P.O. Box 310, Shippensburg, PA 17257-0310

This book and all other Destiny Image's books are available at Christian bookstores and distributors worldwide.

For Worldwide Distribution.

Reach us on the Internet: www.destinyimage.com.

ISBN 13 TP: 9798881504564

ISBN 13 eBook: 9798881504571

CONTENTS

INTRODUCTION

🙙🙖

Introduction to the Summary of "How to Hear God's Voice for Healing"

In a world where physical and emotional wounds abound, the divine call to healing is more relevant than ever. "How to Hear God's Voice for Healing" is a spiritual guide designed to equip believers with the understanding and tools necessary to access divine guidance and healing power. This book delves into the foundational biblical principles and personal disciplines that facilitate a profound connection with God, revealing how this relationship is essential not only for personal wholeness but also for ministering healing to others.

The journey through this book is an invitation to transform the ordinary interactions of daily life into extraordinary encounters with the voice of God. Readers are guided step by step in developing their spiritual senses to recognize and respond to the divine whispers that direct, comfort, and empower. The core message is clear: healing comes from deeply listening to the Holy Spirit, who speaks life and restoration into our brokenness.

This summary aims to distill the key concepts and practical applications from the book to provide a concise reference for those seeking to deepen their ability to hear from God specifically in the context of healing. Whether you are new to the concept of hearing God's voice or looking to refine your spiritual acuity, this guide offers valuable insights that align with the heart of God's promise for healing and restoration.

In these pages, you will find not only the theological underpinnings of divine communication but also actionable steps and real-life examples that demonstrate the power of aligning one's life with God's spoken word. The process of hearing God's voice for healing is demystified, showing that it is accessible to every believer, regardless of their spiritual maturity or background.

As we embark on this summary journey, our prayer is that you will not only understand the principles shared but also experience the reality of God's voice in your life, leading you to greater health, deeper spiritual insights, and an empowered ministry of healing to those around you. Welcome to a transformative exploration of how to hear God's voice for healing—a journey that promises to renew the mind, heal the heart, and revitalize the soul.

CHAPTER 1

TESTIMONIES OF VARIOUS WAYS GOD HEALS

Bible Verse

"He sent His word and healed them, and delivered them from their destructions." - Psalm 107:20 (NKJV)

Introduction

This chapter delves into the diverse methods through which God heals, challenging the common belief that divine healing must always be instantaneous. By sharing personal testimonies and scriptural insights, it invites readers to open their hearts to the various ways God may choose to provide healing, emphasizing the importance of cooperation with divine guidance.

Word of Wisdom

"Be vigilant! We are partners in this

walk. This means you are required to do your part." - Jesus

Main Theme

The main theme of this chapter is the exploration of both instantaneous miracles and process healing as valid forms of divine healing, emphasizing that God's methods are multifaceted and tailored to individual needs.

Key Points

- Healing can be instantaneous or a gradual process, and both are valid expressions of God's power.
- Lack of immediate healing does not necessarily indicate a lack of faith or presence of sin.
- Active participation in one's health is crucial; it involves compliance and submission to God's guidance.
- Emotional and spiritual roots often underlie physical ailments, requiring forgiveness and inner healing.
- Continuous learning and adapting one's lifestyle play a significant role in maintaining health and facilitating healing.
- Divine revelation is key to understanding and removing the barriers to healing.

Key Themes

- **Embracing Both Forms of Healing:** The chapter argues against the limited view of healing as solely instantaneous, illustrating through personal stories how God also heals progressively, guiding individuals through a journey of health restoration.

- **The Role of Personal Responsibility:** Highlighting stories like Linda Garmon's and Uta Milewski's, the chapter teaches that personal choices and compliance with divine instructions are vital in walking out the healing process, which often includes lifestyle changes and embracing spiritual disciplines.
- **Spiritual Roots of Physical Issues:** Through anecdotes such as the woman healed of neck pain after forgiving someone, the chapter shows how addressing emotional and spiritual issues can lead to physical healing, advocating for inner healing as part of the healing process.
- **The Importance of Continuous Learning:** Uta Milewski's story exemplifies how continuous learning about health, embracing new practices, and adapting to one's body's needs can lead to significant improvements in chronic conditions.
- **Healing Through Divine Revelation:** The chapter emphasizes the importance of seeking and acting on divine revelation, as God often provides specific guidance on the steps needed for healing, which may include unconventional methods.
- **Community and Support in Healing:** Testimonies within the chapter reveal that healing often happens in community

settings, such as church groups or through the support of friends and family, highlighting the importance of a supportive network in the healing journey.

Conclusion

This chapter compellingly argues that healing is a multifaceted gift from God, manifesting in both instantaneous miracles and gradual processes. It encourages readers to remain open to God's leading, to actively participate in their own healing journey, and to embrace the comprehensive approach to health God offers. Through these testimonies and teachings, readers are reminded that their healing journey is a personal walk with God, requiring their active engagement and faithfulness to His guidance.

CHAPTER 2

INSTANTANEOUS MIRACLES VERSUS PROCESS HEALING

Bible Verse

"He said, 'If you listen carefully to the voice of the Lord your God and do what is right in his eyes, if you pay attention to his commands and keep all his decrees, I will not bring on you any of the diseases I brought on the Egyptians, for I am the Lord, who heals you.'" - Exodus 15:26 (NIV)

Introduction

This chapter explores the nuanced biblical language around healing, emphasizing the diversity in the methods through which God heals—whether instantaneously or through a process. It invites a deeper understanding of scriptural terms and encourages an open attitude toward the various ways God might choose to work healing in our lives.

Word of Wisdom

"Do whatever is in your power to walk in divine health, rather than depending on divine healing." - Jesus

Main Theme

The distinction between instantaneous miracles and process healing is highlighted, with an exploration of the Greek words *dunamis* and *semeion* for miracles and *iaomai* and *therapeuo* for healing, illustrating how the biblical text supports a spectrum of divine interventions.

Key Points

- The Greek word *dunamis* often translated as "power," is sometimes interpreted as "miracle," emphasizing the might of God rather than the miraculous itself.
- *Iaomai* refers to healing that is sometimes immediate, powered by divine energy, highlighting unique, standout moments of healing in the scriptures.
- *Therapeuo* often suggests a therapeutic process, indicative of a journey toward health that might include various modalities like anointing with oil or herbal remedies.
- The biblical narrative may omit certain details about healing, suggesting that not all healings were instantaneous but some were gradual.

- Healing modalities are varied and can include spiritual, emotional, and physical processes, emphasizing the comprehensive approach God uses to restore health.

Key Themes

- **Scriptural Definitions and Translations:** Understanding the original Greek words for healing and miracle in the Bible (*dunamis, semeion, iaomai, therapeuo*) reveals that scripture recognizes both instantaneous miracles and ongoing processes. This understanding can broaden our expectations and receptivity to how God works.
- **The Healing Process:** The discussion on *therapeuo* and *iaomai* shows that healing in the Bible is not always instant; often, it involves a process that includes physical remedies, emotional forgiveness, and spiritual healing, suggesting a holistic approach to health.
- **Emotional and Spiritual Roots:** Many physical ailments have emotional or spiritual roots, and addressing these through forgiveness and inner healing can lead to physical relief and restoration, as illustrated by personal testimonies.
- **The Importance of Details:** The gospels may not always provide full details of healing stories, indicating that some healings were gradual processes rather than immediate miracles, which encourages

patients and perseverance in our faith journey.

- **Integrative Healing Practices:** The use of natural remedies such as essential oils and herbal treatments in the context of *therapeuo* illustrates the Bible's acknowledgment of various healing practices that can complement spiritual healing.

Conclusion

This chapter underscores the rich and varied ways in which God can heal, from the instantaneous to the progressive. It encourages a deeper dive into scripture to understand the full spectrum of healing, inviting believers to embrace both miraculous events and the healing journey as parts of a divine strategy for restoration and health. Understanding the biblical language of healing helps to set realistic and faithful expectations for how God may choose to work in our lives, emphasizing that both sudden miracles and gradual recoveries manifest His power and purpose.

CHAPTER 3

FAITH AND LOVE: IMPORTANT KEYS TO EXPERIENCING DUNAMIS POWER

Bible Verse

"And though I have all faith, so that I could remove mountains, but have not love, I am nothing." - 1 Corinthians 13:2 (NKJV)

Introduction

This chapter delves into the essential roles of faith and love in activating the dunamis power of God for healing, both miraculous and therapeutic. It explores how the presence or absence of these elements can impact the flow of God's power in healing processes.

Word of Wisdom

"Faith energized by love is the conduit through which the miracle-working power of God flows."

Main Theme

The chapter emphasizes that both faith and love are crucial for the manifestation of God's miracle-working power, illustrating how their presence or absence influenced the healing ministry of Jesus and how they can affect modern-day believers.

Key Points

- Therapeuo healing includes a variety of remedies and can sometimes be instantaneous, showing the diverse ways God heals.
- In His hometown, Jesus encountered unbelief and lack of love, which restricted His ability to perform dunamis miracles, though He could still perform therapeuo healings.
- Historical and biblical examples demonstrate that therapeutic healing can involve natural remedies, such as fasting, which promotes physical health.
- Faith working through love is essential for releasing dunamis power; absence of these elements hinders miraculous healing.
- Inner alignment with God's word and spirit enhances the flow of healing power, affecting both the individual's well-being and their ability to minister healing to others.

Key Themes

- **The Necessity of Faith and Love:** The absence of faith and love in Jesus' hometown limited His miracle-working abilities, teaching that unbelief and resentment can block the flow of divine power. Faith and love must be actively present to fully engage with the dunamis power of God.

- **Therapeuo vs. Dunamis Healing:** The chapter differentiates between therapeuo (process or therapeutic healing) and dunamis (instantaneous miracle) healing. It clarifies that while both can occur, the environment of faith and love greatly influences the type of healing that manifests.
- **Influence of Emotional and Spiritual Health:** Emotional and spiritual health, such as having a joyful heart or a spirit of forgiveness, can have tangible effects on physical health and are integral to the healing process.
- **Role of Natural and Spiritual Remedies:** Natural remedies like fasting and laughter are validated biblically as part of the healing process, which can also include more direct spiritual interventions such as deliverance or the laying on of hands.
- **Comprehensive Approach to Healing:** A holistic approach to healing, incorporating both natural and supernatural elements, is advocated. This approach underscores the importance of aligning one's inner life with God's principles to facilitate healing.

Conclusion

Faith and love are not just spiritual concepts but are practical necessities for accessing the full spectrum of God's healing power. By fostering environments where faith and love thrive, believers can experience both miraculous and therapeutic healings more profoundly. This chapter encourages believers to cultivate these vital attributes not only for personal health but also to effectively minister healing to others.

CHAPTER 4

GET IN SPIRIT

Bible Verse

"But you are not in the flesh but in the Spirit, if indeed the Spirit of God dwells in you." - Romans 8:9 (NKJV)

Introduction

This chapter explores the critical importance of being 'in the Spirit' to effectively harness God's dunamis healing power. It emphasizes that being tuned to one's spirit, coupled with faith and expressing love, are foundational for accessing this divine energy.

Word of Wisdom

"Being in the Spirit involves hearing what God is saying, seeing what He is doing, and feeling the flow of divine energy pulsating through you."

· · ·

Main Theme

The main theme centers on the necessity of being aligned with the Holy Spirit to experience and facilitate God's healing power. The chapter offers practical steps for entering and maintaining a state of being 'in the Spirit' as a regular practice for believers.

Key Points

- Being 'in the Spirit' is vital for accessing God's power and must be as simple as a child's approach.
- Faith is fueled by hearing and seeing what God reveals.
- Love is fueled by perceiving and feeling God's compassion toward all.
- Western rationalism often clashes with biblical injunctions to live by the Spirit rather than by intellect alone.
- Both intuitive and analytical believers can learn to tune into the Spirit and apply its flow in their daily lives.

Key Themes

- **Cultural and Biblical Worldviews Collide:** The Western emphasis on rationalism and intellect often conflicts with the biblical instruction to live by the Spirit. This chapter advocates for a major shift towards a heart-led lifestyle, relying on spiritual intuition as guided by the Holy Spirit.

- **Practical Steps to Being in the Spirit:** Simple, actionable steps such as quieting oneself, seeking visions, tuning into the flow of the Spirit, and journaling are outlined to help believers enter and stay in the Spirit, making it accessible and practical for everyday life.
- **The Role of Faith and Love in Healing:** Faith and love are not just emotional states but spiritual positions that enhance the believer's capacity to receive and minister healing. Their absence was noted to hinder even Jesus' ability to perform miracles in certain contexts.
- **Integration of Heart and Mind:** Encourages an integration of heart and mind, where spiritual insights lead and intellectual understanding follows, which enhances the believer's ability to live out the full potential of their faith.
- **Lifestyle of Spiritual Dependence:** Emphasizes the continuous practice of living in the Spirit, suggesting that this should become a lifestyle rather than an occasional practice, which can transform mundane existence into a life filled with divine encounters and miracles.

Conclusion

'Get in Spirit' challenges believers to cultivate a deep, consistent spiritual life that aligns with the flow of the Holy Spirit. By embracing a lifestyle of being 'in the Spirit,' believers can unlock a more profound experience of God's power, leading to effective ministry and personal transformation. This chapter serves as both a call to spiritual depth and a practical guide to achieving it.

CHAPTER 5

KINGDOM EMOTIONS PRODUCE KINGDOM HEALTH

Bible Verse

"A joyful heart is good medicine, but a crushed spirit dries up the bones." - Proverbs 17:22 (ESV)

Introduction

This chapter challenges the view of emotions as merely soulish and unreliable, presenting them instead as vital to spiritual health and effective healing, embedded within the framework of Kingdom principles.

Word of Wisdom

"Emotions are at the root of most illness; understanding this can transform our approach to healing."

Main Theme

The main theme is the crucial role that emotions play in physical health and spiritual well-being, advocating for the embrace of Kingdom emotions like joy, peace, and love, which enhance immune function and overall health.

Key Points

- Emotions are integral to our spiritual and physical health.
- Negative emotions like fear and unforgiveness can lead to physical ailments.
- Positive Kingdom emotions boost the immune system and promote healing.
- The Bible links physical health directly with emotional and spiritual states.
- Managing emotions according to biblical principles leads to improved health.

Key Themes

- **The Power of Positive Emotions:** Embracing emotions such as joy, peace, and gratitude, which are aspects of the fruit of the Spirit, activates the body's immune system and promotes healing, contrasting sharply with negative emotions that impair health.
- **Biblical Validation of Emotional Impact:** The scriptures provide clear

evidence that our emotional state affects our physical health, with numerous examples showing how positive emotional states are linked to physical healing and wellbeing.

- **Transformation Through Emotional Alignment:** By aligning our emotional life with Kingdom values such as forgiveness and love, we not only obey biblical mandates but also tap into God's design for holistic health.
- **Practical Steps for Emotional Healing:** The chapter offers concrete steps for dealing with negative emotions, including forgiveness and releasing stress through spiritual practices, highlighting the importance of handling emotions biblically.
- **Long-term Emotional Management:** It stresses the importance of continuously managing emotions to maintain spiritual and physical health, suggesting that habitual reformation towards positive emotional states is essential for lasting health.

Conclusion

'Kingdom Emotions Produce Kingdom Health' underscores the profound connection between our emotional state and our physical health, framed within a biblical context. It calls for a radical reevaluation of how we perceive and manage our emotions, promoting a life led by the Spirit to foster both spiritual growth and physical healing.

This chapter serves as both a theological reflection and a practical guide to cultivating health through the fruits of the Spirit.

CHAPTER 6

RELATIONAL FIVE-STEP PRAYER MODEL BY JOHN WIMBER

Bible Verse

"Truly I say to you, whoever says to this mountain, 'Be taken up and cast into the sea,' and does not doubt in his heart, but believes that what he says is going to happen, it will be granted him." - Mark 11:23 (NASB)

Introduction

This chapter explores John Wimber's five-step prayer model for healing, emphasizing the power of heart-level prayers and their effectiveness in addressing both physical and spiritual ailments.

Word of Wisdom

"Prayers are most effective when applied directly to the point when the hurt happened."

Main Theme

The main theme focuses on the transformative power of the five-step prayer model developed by John Wimber, which integrates emotional, spiritual, and physical healing through structured, heart-level engagement.

Key Points

- Heart-level prayers engage emotions, imagination, and spiritual flow.
- Forgiveness is a crucial component of effective prayer.
- The five-step model includes interview, diagnosis, prayer ministry, re-interview, and post-prayer instructions.
- Healing often involves addressing root causes related to emotional or generational issues.
- Continuous feedback during prayer sessions enhances the healing process.

Key Themes

- **Integration of Heart and Spirit in Prayer:** By focusing on the heart's language—flowing thoughts, pictures, and emotions—prayers tap into deeper spiritual realities, enhancing the prayer's impact and fostering profound healing connections.

- **Forgiveness as a Gateway to Healing:** The act of forgiveness, especially when visualized and felt deeply, is presented as essential in healing prayers, serving as a spiritual release and a pathway to physical and emotional healing.
- **Structured Prayer Approach:** Wimber's model provides a systematic approach to spiritual healing that involves thorough engagement with the recipient's history and current spiritual state, encouraging a holistic view of health and spiritual well-being.
- **Dynamic Interaction in Prayer:** The model emphasizes ongoing interaction and adaptation during the prayer process, allowing for real-time adjustments based on the recipient's responses, which helps in targeting the prayers more effectively.
- **Sustainability of Healing:** Post-prayer practices are crucial for maintaining the healing and spiritual growth achieved during the prayer sessions, including continuous self-examination and spiritual discipline.

Conclusion

The chapter outlines a robust framework for conducting healing prayers that is both relational and deeply spiritual. It emphasizes the necessity of integrating emotional healing with spiritual practices, using Wimber's five-step model to guide individuals towards lasting health and spiritual growth. This approach not only addresses immediate physical ailments but also encourages a sustained spiritual journey towards healing and wholeness.

CHAPTER 7

WORDS OF KNOWLEDGE INCREASE THE FAITH LEVEL

Bible Verse

"Truly I say to you, whoever says to this mountain, 'Be taken up and cast into the sea,' and does not doubt in his heart, but believes that what he says is going to happen, it will be granted him." – Mark 11:23 (NASB)

Introduction

This chapter explores how words of knowledge can significantly increase faith levels during healing services, facilitating miraculous healings and deepening believers' trust in God's direct intervention.

Word of Wisdom

"Be cautious in how you present what you believe you are receiving from God. Speak with humility, recognizing that you are still learning to hear His voice."

Main Theme

Words of knowledge are spiritual insights revealed by God to specifically target and heal physical ailments, effectively increasing faith and prompting divine healing.

Key Points

• Words of knowledge can manifest as physical sensations, visions, or spontaneous thoughts that indicate God's healing intention.

• Expressing these insights during services can lead to instant healings, reinforcing the power of faith.

• Spiritual sensitivity is required to receive and deliver words of knowledge appropriately.

• Maintaining humility when sharing prophetic insights ensures a respectful and effective ministry.

• Continuous learning and spiritual growth are essential for mastering the delivery of words of knowledge.

• Collaborative prayer enhances the healing process, affirming the collective faith of the community.

Key Themes

• **Mechanisms of Receiving Words of Knowledge:** God communicates healing needs through various channels such as physical sensations in the minister's body, mental images, or specific words that suddenly come to mind. Recognizing these signals requires a deep attunement to the Holy Spirit's promptings.

- **Impact of Words of Knowledge on Faith and Healing:** When a minister accurately shares a word of knowledge, it dramatically increases the faith of the recipient, often resulting in immediate and miraculous healings. This dynamic showcases the direct involvement of Jesus in the healing process.
- **Guidelines for Delivering Words of Knowledge:** Delivering a word of knowledge should be done with humility and care, using clear, relatable language. Ministers should encourage recipients to accept the word if it resonates, but also to feel free to dismiss it if it does not align with their spirit.
- **Developing Prophetic Sensitivity and Integrity:** Those practicing this gift must cultivate a sensitive and ethical approach, ensuring that their words do not coerce or manipulate but rather invite recipients to connect more deeply with God.
- **The Role of Community and Continuous Learning:** Developing the gift of prophecy and words of knowledge is enhanced through community interaction and ongoing spiritual mentorship. Learning from experienced ministers and engaging in reflective practice are crucial for growth.

Conclusion

Words of knowledge are powerful tools in the ministry of healing, directly enhancing the faith of believers and facilitating divine interventions. By responsibly developing and utilizing this gift, ministers can profoundly impact individuals' lives, demonstrating God's love and power in tangible ways.

CHAPTER 8

PRACTICAL GUIDELINES AS WE MINISTER HEALING

Bible Verse

"But the path of the righteous is like the light of dawn, that shines brighter and brighter until the full day." – Proverbs 4:18 (NASB)

Introduction

This chapter delves into actionable, biblically-rooted strategies for effective healing ministry, emphasizing the transition from flesh to Spirit to foster true healing and spiritual growth.

Word of Wisdom

"The more practical we can be, the easier it is for a person to follow the steps and move forward to victory."

Main Theme

The chapter outlines specific, practical steps for transitioning into and sustaining spiritual healing practices, guided by biblical principles and a deep connection with the Holy Spirit.

Key Points

• Unconditional love is fundamental to effective healing.

• Fear and doubt block healing, while joy and love facilitate it.

• Engage deeply with the Holy Spirit to guide the healing process.

• Visualize healing as a full-body experience, addressing each part consciously.

• Group healing sessions can magnify the healing power through collective faith.

• Embrace continuous spiritual refilling to maintain healing efficacy.

Key Themes

• **Transitioning from Flesh to Spirit:** Moving from flesh-driven reactions to Spirit-led responses involves disconnecting from worldly influences and connecting deeply with the Holy Spirit. This connection is visualized as the flow of God's energy through thoughts, visions, and emotions.

- **The Importance of Emotion in Healing:** Emotions like joy and gratitude not only enhance the healing environment but are also crucial in carrying the healing power. Practitioners must cultivate these emotions genuinely to effectively minister healing.
- **Visualization Techniques in Healing:** Visualizing specific biblical and spiritual images can significantly boost faith and the effectiveness of healing prayers. These visual aids help practitioners and patients focus on the divine power at work.
- **Group Dynamics in Healing:** Group soaking prayer sessions, where multiple individuals focus their spiritual energy and prayer on one person, have shown to be powerful. The collective faith and concentrated prayer intensify the healing process.
- **Practical Steps for Healing Sessions:** Detailed steps such as assessing the patient's condition, tuning into the Spirit, and continuously observing the healing process are vital. These steps ensure that the healing session is thorough and attuned to the Spirit's movement.

Conclusion

The chapter provides a comprehensive guide to conducting healing sessions that are spiritually potent and practically effective. By focusing on spiritual connectivity and practical steps, practitioners can facilitate profound healing and witness miraculous recoveries, ultimately glorifying God through their ministry.

CHAPTER 9

PEG YARBROUGH'S SPIRIT-LED APPROACH TO HEALING

Bible Verse

"When Jesus had called the Twelve together, he gave them power and authority to drive out all demons and to cure diseases, and he sent them out to proclaim the kingdom of God and to heal the sick." – Luke 9:1-2 (NIV)

Introduction

In this chapter, Rev. Peg Yarbrough shares her Spirit-led methodology for healing, emphasizing the importance of a personal and adaptable approach that engages both healer and recipient in a deeply spiritual process.

Word of Wisdom

"You cannot rush Jesus at work."

Main Theme

Focusing on the individuality of each healing experience, Rev. Yarbrough outlines seven steps that blend spiritual depth with practical actions, ensuring that each session is led by the Spirit and tailored to the recipient's needs.

Key Points

• Start each session with an opening prayer inviting Jesus's presence and protection.

• Build trust with the recipient to facilitate open and honest communication.

• Engage the atmosphere of high faith in large meetings to quicken healing.

• Address deeper issues progressively, peeling back layers like an onion.

• Always let Jesus guide the healing process, using the practitioner as a facilitator.

• Maintain a judgment-free stance with unconditional love and patience.

• Emphasize continuous engagement with Jesus to ensure effective healing.

Key Themes

• **Building Trust and Atmosphere:** Trust is crucial for effective healing; it allows individuals to open up and participate fully in their healing process. In larger settings, the collective faith can enhance the speed and visibility of healing outcomes.

- **The Role of Deep Emotional and Spiritual Work:** Healing is often more than just physical; it involves addressing deep-seated emotional and spiritual wounds. This process can be lengthy and requires patience, with the healer acting as a guide rather than a director.
- **Importance of Continuous Spiritual Engagement:** Consistent and ongoing engagement with the Holy Spirit is essential. Practitioners must remain connected to divine guidance throughout the healing process, ensuring that each step is Spirit-led.
- **Visualization and the Power of Imagination:** Visualizing positive outcomes and spiritual presence plays a critical role in the healing process. This approach helps both the healer and the recipient focus on the potential for divine intervention.
- **Flexibility and Adaptability in Healing:** Each healing session is unique and must be tailored to the individual's specific spiritual and emotional needs. This adaptive approach helps address the root causes of ailments more effectively.

Conclusion

Rev. Peg Yarbrough's approach to healing underscores the need for a flexible, compassionate, and Spirit-led methodology that respects the uniqueness of each individual's journey towards healing. By maintaining a focus on Jesus and allowing Him to lead, healers can facilitate profound spiritual and physical restoration.

CHAPTER 10

A SPIRIT-LED PROTOCOL FOR CLAIMING GOD'S PROMISES

Bible Verse

"Many will say to Me on that day, 'Lord, Lord, did we not prophesy in Your name, and in Your name cast out demons, and in Your name perform many miracles?' And then I will declare to them, 'I never knew [ginosko] you; depart from Me, you who practice lawlessness.'" - Matthew 7:22-23 (NASB95)

Introduction

This chapter explores the profound spiritual approach to claiming God's promises, emphasizing the necessity of seeking divine guidance and cultivating a relationship with God rather than mechanically applying biblical promises.

Word of Wisdom

"Do not do anything on your own,

and yes, that even includes claiming My promises."

Main Theme

The chapter outlines a Spirit-led protocol for engaging with God's promises, focusing on the interaction between personal intimacy with God and the application of His Word.

Key Points

• Engage directly with God to understand and apply His promises.

• Seek God's counsel to ensure promises are applied correctly.

• Recognize the importance of a personal relationship over mechanical recitation of Scripture.

• Acknowledge that true spiritual power comes from intimacy with God, not mere knowledge.

• Understand that God desires a fellowship and communion that influences how promises are claimed.

• Embrace the process of spiritual intimacy as a way to deeply connect with God's purposes.

Key Themes

• **Personal Engagement with Scripture:** Claiming God's promises involves more than reciting verses; it requires a dialogue with God to understand His intentions and timing. This process ensures that the application of His Word is both meaningful and personally tailored.

- **The Importance of Intimacy over Mechanism:** True spiritual effectiveness arises not from the mechanical use of God's Word but through a deep, relational understanding with God. This intimacy transforms how promises are perceived and applied, moving beyond formulaic practices to a dynamic interaction with the Divine.

- **Role of the Holy Spirit in Claiming Promises:** The Holy Spirit acts as a guide in selecting and applying Scripture, highlighting the need for believers to rely on divine insight rather than personal selection of promises. This guidance ensures that the application of Scripture aligns with God's specific purposes for an individual's life.

- **Misuse of Spiritual Power:** The danger of exercising spiritual gifts without intimacy with God is highlighted, stressing that miraculous powers in themselves do not equate to righteousness or salvation. This serves as a caution against the commodification of divine promises.

- **Fellowship as the Foundation for Spiritual Authority:** Emphasizing fellowship with God underscores the necessity for believers to cultivate a relationship where spiritual authority is not merely about power but about walking in communion with God. This approach ensures that the use of God's promises is infused with love, wisdom, and genuine spiritual insight.

Conclusion

The chapter concludes by reiterating the necessity of seeking a heartfelt, intimate relationship with God when claiming His promises. It argues that this approach not only aligns with biblical teaching but also deepens the believer's spiritual life, ensuring that the promises of God are manifested in a context of love, intimacy, and divine guidance.

CHAPTER 11

TWENTY-EIGHT THERAPEUTIC HEALING PROTOCOLS

Bible Verse

"God has appointed in the church... gifts of healings" - 1 Corinthians 12:28 (NASB95)

Introduction

This chapter provides an extensive overview of 28 therapeutic healing modalities that align with scriptural principles, offering Christians confidence in integrating these practices into their health routines without compromising their faith.

Word of Wisdom

"No, we gauge things by whether they are compatible with Scripture, produce life, and the Spirit of Truth within us affirms this is a direction we are to go in."

Main Theme

Exploring diverse and biblically sound therapeutic modalities, this chapter encourages believers to embrace holistic approaches to health that harmonize with spiritual convictions and biblical truths.

Key Points

• Therapeutic healing aligns with the gifts of healings referenced in the scriptures.

• True healing often involves a process, not just instantaneous results.

• Modalities include deliverance, inner healing, breaking curses, and using herbs.

• Each therapy is vetted for compatibility with Scripture and effectiveness in promoting life.

• Believers are encouraged to engage actively with these practices under the guidance of the Holy Spirit.

Key Themes

- **Compatibility with Scripture:** Each therapeutic modality presented is scrutinized for its alignment with biblical principles, ensuring that they support a life-giving, Christ-centered approach to healing.
- **Role of the Holy Spirit:** The chapter underscores the importance of the Holy Spirit in guiding believers to select and

properly apply therapeutic modalities, emphasizing reliance on divine direction rather than mere human judgment.

- **Embracing Comprehensive Healing Approaches:** The modalities range from spiritual practices like deliverance and inner healing to natural remedies such as herbs and laughter, promoting a holistic approach to health that respects both spiritual and physical aspects of well-being.
- **Importance of Forgiveness and Emotional Release:** Therapies that involve forgiveness and releasing emotional burdens are highlighted as particularly effective, demonstrating the deep connection between spiritual well-being and physical health.
- **Continuous Engagement and Personal Responsibility:** The chapter advocates for an active, persistent pursuit of health, encouraging readers to continually seek God's guidance and apply various healing protocols until full health is achieved.

Conclusion

By presenting a range of therapeutic healing protocols, this chapter empowers believers to actively pursue health and wellness in a manner that is both spiritually fulfilling and biblically sound. It encourages a proactive approach to health, guided by the Holy Spirit and grounded in Scripture, enabling Christians to live out their faith confidently in every aspect of their lives.

CHAPTER 12

PLANTED BY THE RIVER AND BEARING FRUIT CONTINUALLY

Bible Verse

"Then he showed me a river of the water of life, clear as crystal, coming from the throne of God and of the Lamb, in the middle of its street. On either side of the river was the tree of life, bearing twelve kinds of fruit, yielding its fruit every month; and the leaves of the tree were for the healing of the nations." - Revelation 22:1-2 NASB95

Introduction

This chapter vividly describes a Spirit-anointed lifestyle as living continually nourished by the 'river of the water of life,' a metaphor for an abundant life filled with divine influence through the Holy Spirit. The imagery drawn from Revelation provides a template for understanding how Christians can thrive spiritually by staying connected to divine sources.

Word of Wisdom

"Abiding in Christ is the only meaningful lifestyle. It is worth taking the time to fully master this lifestyle."

Main Theme

The chapter explores the dynamics of a Spirit-anointed life, characterized by a deep, continuous connection to the spiritual nourishment provided by God. It outlines how living in sync with the Holy Spirit not only brings personal renewal but also empowers believers to bear fruit in every season of their lives.

Key Points

• Living by the Holy Spirit requires continuous immersion in God's presence, characterized by a flow of divine ideas, emotions, and energies.

• Understanding and applying the laws of the Spirit can transform our everyday experiences, aligning them more closely with God's purposes.

• The analogy of water and wind as sources of power illustrates how spiritual truths can be harnessed for abundant living.

• Practical steps for engaging with the Holy Spirit include quieting oneself, envisioning Jesus' presence, and actively receiving His guidance through spiritual flow.

• God uses both gentle whispers and profound revelations to guide us, emphasizing the need for a balanced, attentive spiritual life.

• Embracing a Spirit-led life involves daily decisions to rely on divine insight rather than human reasoning.

Key Themes

- • **Spiritual Laws and Definitions:** Precise definitions of spiritual laws, akin to physical laws like gravity, help believers understand and navigate their spiritual journeys effectively. These laws are not just theological concepts but practical truths that can lead to a powerful, Spirit-filled life.
- • **The Power of Imagery:** Visualizing spiritual truths, such as the river of life and the tree bearing fruit, plays a crucial role in internalizing and living out biblical principles. This mental imagery helps shift focus from worldly concerns to divine promises and interventions.
- **Flow of the Spirit:** Living in the 'flow' involves a shift from self-directed effort to Spirit-led spontaneity in thoughts, actions, and words. This transition is essential for experiencing the fullness of life that Jesus promises to His followers.
- **Harnessing Spiritual Power:** Just as mankind has learned to harness natural elements for energy, believers are called to harness spiritual dynamics for transformation and healing. This includes

recognizing and operating in the flow of the Holy Spirit to release divine power in their lives.

- **Integration of Spiritual Practices:** Daily spiritual disciplines, such as prayer, meditation on Scripture, and two-way journaling, are vital for maintaining a deep connection with God. These practices ensure that believers remain rooted and grounded in love, growing in faith and obedience.
- **Transformation through Abiding:** The core message of abiding in Christ involves a continual, intimate relationship with Him, which transforms believers from the inside out. This spiritual process is marked by an increasing alignment with God's will and character.

Conclusion

Chapter 12 of "Planted by the River and Bearing Fruit Continually" serves as a profound reminder of the transformative power of living a life deeply rooted in the Holy Spirit. It challenges believers to immerse themselves in the divine flow of God's presence, harnessing His power to bear fruit in every season. As believers align their lives with these spiritual principles, they experience continuous growth, healing, and effectiveness in their Christian walk, fulfilling their God-given potential and purpose.